To Steve

My Husband's Eyebrows is
a collection of illustrated poetry
primarily about my long marriage—
the good, the bad and the ugly, of course—
the warmth
the mundane
the hilarity
doubt
love
the disappointments
astonishment
boredom
the joy.

You know.
Full spectrum.

My Husband's Eyebrows

An Illustrated Chapbook
by
Leanne Grabel

A Publication of The Poetry Box®

Editing & Book Design by Shawn Aveningo Sanders
Illustrations by Leanne Grabel
Cover Design & "Stage" Illustration by Robert R. Sanders

ISBN: 978-1-956285-25-3
Printed in the United States of America.
Wholesale Distribution by Ingram Group

Published by The Poetry Box®, October 25, 2022
Portland, Oregon
https://thepoetrybox.com

I may go crazy before that mansion on the hill.

—Van Morrison

Contents

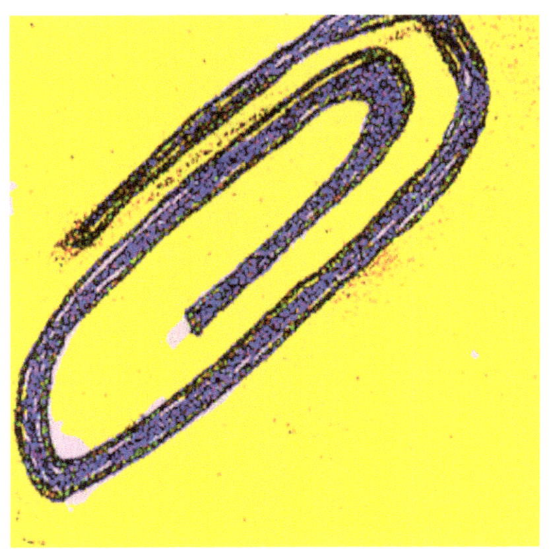

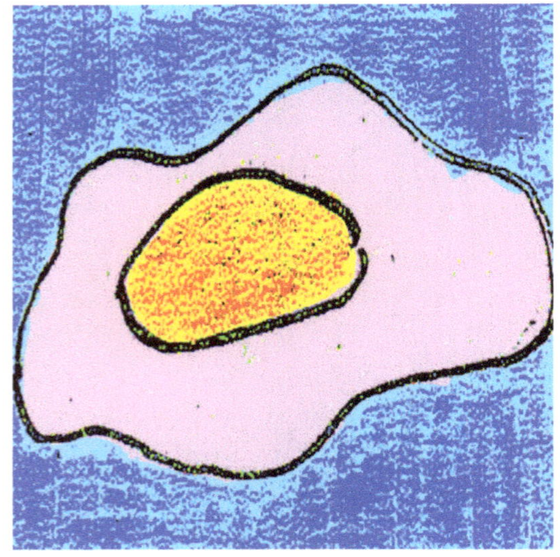

Exactly

You settle upon the
knobs on the dresser drawer,
you decide that the secret is there.
—Charles Bukowski

I feel an epiphany coming on
as if it's right around the corner
as if I'm just about to turn
and see a paperclip
or a couch cushion
or a fried egg
and I'll know something.

I feel as if a light is going to fall
upon a dense and crotchety shadow.
I'll feel a warmth in my shoulders
and behind my ears
a slight shuffling in my brain
as if a chair moved
in my medulla oblongata.

It might happen any minute.
I'll find a billfold full of hundreds
and antidotes.
I'll take it.
Wouldn't you?
And I'll tell him.
Wouldn't you?

At first, I didn't think I would—
I mean, tell him.
But I would.
And he'll probably say, "What?"
absentmindedly
and I'll get irritated
that he isn't more enthusiastic.

Honey

The night I met my husband, he was wearing an enormous sweater with brown buttons like mini buns. He also had a girlfriend on his arm like an alligator purse. I noticed immediately she was the opposite of me. She was naturally blonde, naturally thin, talkative. Plus, she had on high heels and a powder blue sweater. I was just back from my hometown in California, where I had been watching my grandmother die and trying to mend a cracked heart.

The night I met my husband, I was wearing tight—tight heart, tight spine, tight jeans, tight tank top. My husband started following me around, room to room, after his girlfriend left. He kept telling me things, telling me things. "Love at first sight," he said with his big white teeth like Chiclets. And then he disappeared for a month. "Thanks for your patience and understanding," he said before he left. Impulsive, I didn't really practice, or even understand, patience. But I waited.

We finally made love on a beautiful, tropical, overstuffed couch in the middle of my new rental room in a large Victorian house. The couch was periwinkle blue chintz with splashes of white irises. The room had a balcony ringed by old hawthorns that stood there like sage uncles.

The love was honey. No. It was the taste of honey, the look of honey. No. It was bathing in warmed honey—golden, thick, sweet. I made layered mammalian sounds with panache. I went from kitten to bobcat to tiger. I remember exactly how my teeth shimmied, my paws buzzed. (I mean, my feet.)

It was about a year later when the judges arrived and took their permanent seats in my occipital court. They tried to ruin everything with their snotty little number cards.

Now, thirty-eight years have gone by. My husband and I sit on our brown leather couch like couch pillows. We could probably feed the hungry of a small nation with all the crumbs beneath the cushions.

Someone should vacuum.

JUDGES

On a Scale of One to Ten, Part 1

Dr. Misaka and I talked about joy during my eighth session. She was my psychologist for ten sessions. I'd said the word *rape* on the phone to Kaiser and Kaiser gave me every option there was. I chose Dr. Misaka, psychologist. I could bike to her office.

Dr. Misaka was a small woman, even smaller than I am, which is rare. She had beautiful small shoes. That day they were tiny tie-up booties the color of cognac.

I was hoping she could give me the antidote for chronic fear and anxiety. I'd tried many antidotes, but nothing was really sticking.

At the eighth session, I told Dr. Misaka I felt closer to joy. Of course, she was pleased. Was it true? I don't know. It didn't feel false. I had changed my posture. I was lifting my head. I was waking some mornings with loft.

That day I awoke and thought of gleaming on Lauren, like sprinkling sugar or crushed nuts. We were meeting for lunch after Dr. Misaka. "I lay in bed and imagined gleaming on everyone," I said.

"That's great," said Dr. Misaka, who thought my father's anger was more detrimental to my mental and emotional health than rape. "You're getting free," she said. "There is no one shouting at the head of the table. No one flaming."

She was right. And there was no one chopping onions. Dunes of onions. Enough onions to please him. That large man at the head of the table was always shouting for onions, enough onions to start the whole world crying.

The Question of Sobbing & Shitting

When Bailey died, my husband sobbed in my arms. He rocked and shook. Full-body. I'd never seen this before. In thirty-eight years, I'd seen only a handful of tears, usually after a documentary about a self-destructive artistic genius, like Jean-Michel Basquiat or Miles Davis. But when Bailey died, my husband shook and shivered. (I shook and shivered too but only four times and always after he left for work.)

I know this is not about me. I know my husband keeps secrets. I'm glad (I think). I don't want to know what he does every minute or what he hides at the back of his socks drawer. And I don't want to see him shit. Of course, I've caught a hooded glance or two in passing over the years. But not on purpose. In the end, I don't think I can wipe his ass.

The Unbearable Lightness of Marriage

Sometimes, in the morning, after battling the crude monsters of night, the detritus of their cruel messages like sharp crumbs in my bed, my sheets wrinkled and twisted, pillow lumpy with pummel, I awake and hear my husband, giggling like a child, lapping up the banter of the women on the news. They are nibbling macarons and discussing the difference between macarons and macaroons, as if speaking to toddlers.

It makes me want to grab a rolling pin and pound my husband on the head like Blondie pounded Dagwood until it looks like I baked a berry pie with his head and his brains.

Kidding.

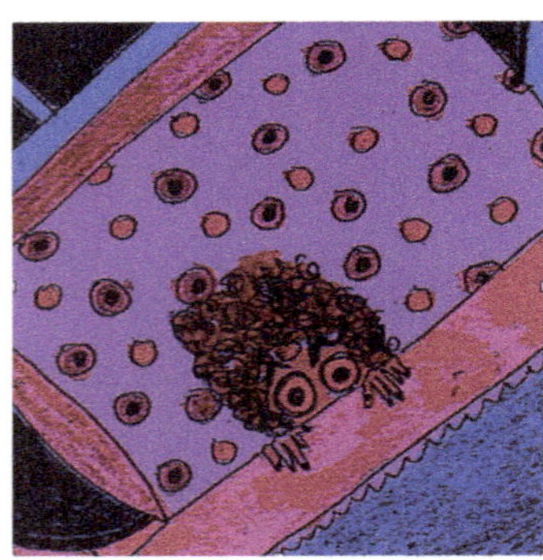

Crocodile

He asked me how my CBD oil supply was doing. I had been rubbing it into my hands, which look like ginger root, which work like ginger root and ache at the knots and knobs (I mean joints). His question annoyed me. What is he? My grandmother? Sometimes my husband's avuncularity feels like lint stuck to my oily face, like long-sleeved silk in summer.

"Don't nurse me," I snapped impatiently.

What is he? My mom? I know. I know I'll regret this later. I always regret my bites. But I'm a crocodile. I snap. Lucky for you, I've lost a few teeth. And the ones I still have are chewed down. The future should be kinder.

Candy

My husband is a master of mimicry. He can imitate any sound that he hears. He can do double sounds, triple sounds. He layers accents, animals, machinery, technology. One day we were walking along the river and he mimicked a Polish Jew with a missing tooth selling hotdogs at a Yankees game. Then over coffee, he mimicked a Frenchman with a lisp, a jaw click and a Chinese accent. I laughed so hard, I felt three. Last month he mimicked radio static. Masterfully. It was exact. Hilarious.

"It's our new song," I said. And we laughed and laughed.

I am grateful for my husband's talents. He could probably mimic the sound of gratitude. But what is it? A sibilant whoosh? A muffled whoopee behind a handkerchief? Mimicry is no talent of mine. My lips are slow-moving (the only part of me that is). And I often don't listen well, as if my ears just get up and go inside.

But when my husband mimics perfectly and we laugh like that, like we're three or eleven or even forty, that's the cream in the center of the bon bon. And candy is absolutely necessary.

VIVA LA
FRANTH.

NY

WHOOSH

GOO

Compare an Orange

 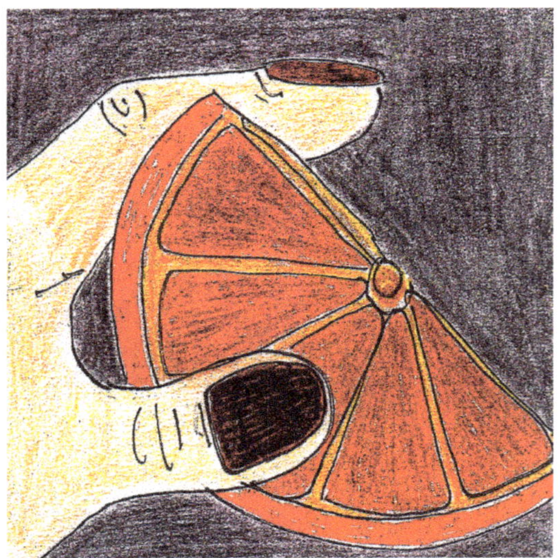

We sit on the couch. (Yes, I feel shame for the staidness.) Around eight, I go get an orange from the fruit bowl. I peel it. I plop the two largest sections into my mouth. Juices squirt out my mouth like citrus whiskers.

O. Oranges. The fruit of my youth.

Boxes and boxes of oranges on the porch. *Maybe I should I ask him if he wants some*, I think. Then I ask him, "Do you want some?" Before he answers, I give him three sections. See? I used to be stingy. So stingy. But I'm heading for generous. Progress is slow. But I'm learning from him, which was the point.

Asparagus Tips

My husband started adding asparagus tips to our egg scrambles after thirty-five years of weekly egg scrambles without them. That's like eighteen hundred egg scrambles and zero asparagus tips . . . until now. Why? I'd been hoping he would change, of course. But I had no idea the change was going to come, nor that it would be culinary.

Now there are families of headless asparagus in the fridge. Green skinny torsos in brown paper pencil skirts. Last week he discovered the neck of the asparagus is as good as the head when sauteed with garlic in ghee. It might even be better, more texture and grit, less goosh. May that be said of my husband.

Convention

What if your husband went to a union convention and came back with a woman who he said was the love of his life, even though he said you were the love of his life . . . BUT, you were glad? What if neither of you thought you were unhappy (or happy) to begin with? What if your faucet had been dripping for thirty years and your husband kept saying he was going to fix it, but he didn't for thirty years? What if he started making stupid sex jokes using plumbing supplies vocabulary like *pipe* and *joint* and *flange*? What if you never realized, for a second, he was a man who would make jokes like that? You hate jokes like that. And you'd never heard him use a plumbing supply term before in your life? What if your husband went to a union convention and didn't come back at all? Would your head spin around in its socket? Would it land in the same place? How many rotations? What if it spun halfway? Would you be looking at yesterday or tomorrow? What if a year passed and your husband came back? Would you be glad?

Not Invited to the Party

Thirty-eight years ago Sunday
I first had coffee with my husband.
I missed his train of thought, but
I loved his driving motivation—
me. It was me.

Now we sit like hassocks—
tattered, mad and innocent.
Some of the china is chipped
even the company saucers.
He must have partied without me.

Prequel

Before Steve, before I married Steve, I was in love with a husband. He was in love with everyone else besides me, maybe me. I wanted him so badly, I wore down two molars and a wisdom tooth. I wanted to share a pillow with him, a tube of toothpaste, a soft-boiled egg in an egg cup. I wanted to wear him like a purse, be his purse, be in his purse.

He said it didn't matter. He said all love ended up the same. "I look at my wife and it's like I've never seen her before in life," he said. "Do you know what I mean? My great uncle touches his wife's ass and can't tell if it's her ass or his." And then he laughed and laughed like a drunk in a sports bar. And it hurt.

I thought we were an important love story, even when he lied a thousand times, even when he told me my pillow smelled that one night he stayed over, but left in the middle of the night. I wept and wept. I made sounds I'd never made before.

Now he's married 48 years and I'm married 36. He's probably had 20 lovers since me, maybe more. Back then he said his wife didn't mind his lovers. Wrong. He asked me if I would. "Yes," I said knowing I was ruining my chances.

Now I kind of know what he meant, though. Last night I bent over to look at my big toe, which was cramping after walking downtown in new shoes, and my husband pulled a muscle in his back.

Is that what he meant?

LIES
OW!

Millionth Crow Poem

I fear birds.
To be frank.
I fear in general.
Fear's how I roll.

So when hundreds of crows
converged upon our lawn
our house, our trees, the block
I feared.

So much flapping and squawking.
The numbers were frightening.
Hitchcockian.
It had to be bad.

"What's up with the crows?"
I yelled at my husband.
Crows were pouring from the pallor
in inky torrents.

"Maybe they're here to warn us," I said.
"Maybe they're kind.
Maybe they like us.
Maybe there's nothing to fear."

It was such a generous assumption
like when I decided cows were kind
so there was no mad cow disease
in every bite of beef I took.

Every branch, every post, every wire
was beaded with crows.
Crows like gems, like jewels.
Black sapphires. Ebon diamonds.

My New Year's resolution
was to be more generous.
Crows like gems, like jewels
is the most generous line
I've ever written.

My Husband's Eyebrows

My husband's eyebrows became electrified in Costa Rica. Anarchistic caterpillars with mohawks. Punks. We called them Syd Vicious throughout the vacation. And we laughed every time. My granddaughter toddled in too-large flippers. She reminded me of Dustin Hoffman in "The Graduate." I laughed every time. Then I nuzzled her. We all nuzzled her. What a tonic.

My daughters and I wore our Polish thighs like trees. They wore theirs with pride, like oaks or redwoods. I wrapped mine in towels. I had decades of experience showing shame, like a peasant or a shrub. The native men wore their shirts unbuttoned. Their bellies bragged. And I liked it, surprisingly. Maybe because they weren't that handsome.

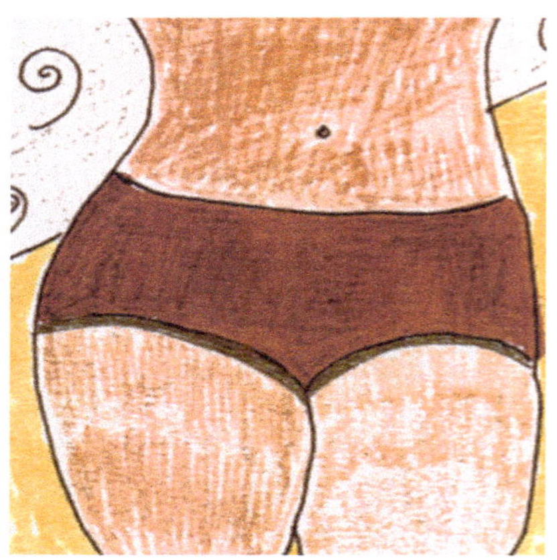

The water in Costa Rica was perfect. There was no difference between water and body and air. Not a flinch. We just lolled in infinity pools drinking pina coladas with bright fans of pineapple, kicking our legs plopped on underwater stools made of volcanic stone.

At breakfast white-faced monkeys like jesters swung above us. They tried hard to charm us. They swooped low and picked up the sugar bowls. Then flaunted their booty. Sugar packets fanned out like large paper dentures. Sugar packets dangled from their ironic smiles. One monkey wore a bowl on his head. Then he dropped all the Splenda on ours. Only the Splenda.

I thought I looked great in Costa Rica, especially for my age. Then I saw the photos. I looked like a peasant from Minsk among Swedes. I was shorter than the others, squatter than the others. My body looked like a potato. My hair, a riot. But for Minsk, I had a singular style. That is what I told myself for consolation.

And anyway, this is a poem about my husband's eyebrows. Not me.

Bald

My husband always says, "Yes." He used to drive carpools, go to soccer games in the rain, basketball games in small muggy gyms with everybody yelling, Chucky Cheese birthday parties. He chaperoned long weeks at outdoor school, class trips to the planetariums and aquariums, and he took our children school shopping the night before the first day of school when the chaos was like inside a blender. Now he goes grocery shopping, takes care of the cast iron pans, empties the dishwasher, carries the heavy stuff. That my husband always says "Yes" is one of the main reasons I married him. And I'm sure it's why our daughters are so generous. In my family, generosity was a foreign idea. Instead, we were pitted against each other, competing. And we were stingy. My husband doesn't have a competitive, nor stingy, cell in his body—except, perhaps, the cells on his head. His hair follicles would rather die than share space with anything

Ass of Lies

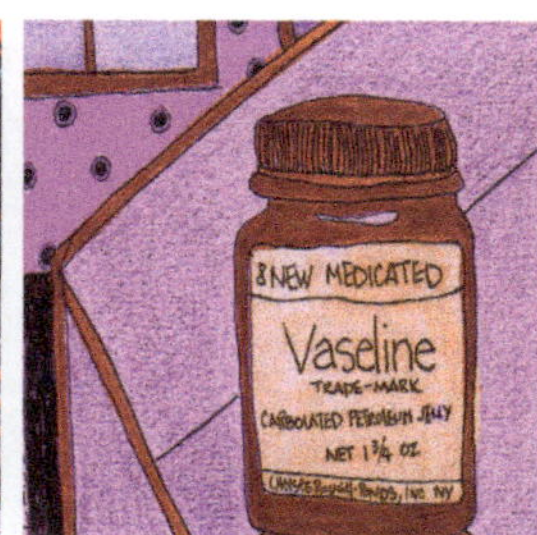

Last week my husband was drunk at a party and said he'd rather fuck me than the blonde in the seersucker dress. She was prancing about with her ass in the air like a bustle.

"You mean the blonde who was named after birds?" I asked. "The blonde with that ass full of lies?"

Not an hour before I had asked him what life with a storm cloud was like.

"You're a fabulous package," he said. And he patted my ass in an ambiguous way.

My malaise and impatience fled straight to the bathroom and started looking through drawers. They found a brown jar of Vaseline, a clot of black bobby pins, a dusty brown hairnet like a nest for a cockroach.

Then today I hennaed my hair orange by mistake. I was going for dark pink, but the cumin overpowered the rooibos tea. My hair *is* as orange as an orange. Orange does nothing for my face. But it is the opposite of what it was before and for some of us, opposition is the lifeblood.

Oy

My husband slogs in hangdog, hangs in slogdog. I scuttle jerkily, elbows first. Both of us sniff for old smells, almost unfamiliar. I inch for the door, going nowhere. He stares out the large picture window. The view is two trees and the school across the street. He says nothing. I say nothing. Our marriage says nothing. It's rough like old stucco.

He fears change like a stroke. I fear tender, fear stasis, hear "mistake, mistake, mistake," a droning in my head like an ache. But I can't hear who's talking and I don't know which mistake. I open the door. The night is entangled in heat. I close the door. Nobody knows what to do.

Theater

Had to
put it
beneath the stage lights.
Had to hire a director.
Had to put him in a dead poet's clothes.
Had to put on a catsuit and slither like a panther.
Had to hire a choir.
Had to hire a saxman.
Had to open my mouth.
Had to put it in my mouth.
Had to want to.

On a Scale from One to Ten, Part 2

"What number would you say your anxiety is now?" Dr. Misaka asked me. "And your depression?"

"Maybe a one or two . . . unless we're talking America or cancer. Then it's off the charts," I said.

Nine months earlier, I'd said they both were a nine.

"Why the one or two?" she asked.

"Because there's just always something unavoidably upsetting, like a nail in the sole of my shoe."

On the ride home, I decided to greet my husband with a kiss. We'd been pecking for decades while grating cheese, roasting kale, growing old. But by the time he got home, I was down in the basement, wiping windows caked in a hundred years of grime. I was rearranging clutter that was older than our grown children.

So now there's a large empty space in the middle of the mottled basement floor. Someone could have a yoga class down there. But who would want to? There are mold spores from the late 19th century down there. They could be valuable, they're so old. And deadly. I'm just happy to see them dying in the new light.

Ghost of Our Lust

I thought I'd never see it again
I mean him in the glint
and the glow of
my hunger, the
decades of socks
the mundane
the annoyance.
Then Tuesday
a bat that was
caught in the rafters
fluttered down with a
flapping and flurry
and I felt a thigh
on his thigh
on my thigh
on his thigh.

Barbarians

In Brueghel's painting of Icarus (and Human Indifference) and Auden's poem about Brueghel's painting of Icarus (and Human Indifference), a boy falls from the sky, but nobody notices.

The ships sail by without a blip or a bump. The dogs graze and forage, wiggle and bark. The torturer's horse scratches its ass against rough trunks.

In the more recent Era of the Ugly Man (and Human Indifference), there was a man in a suit who was shouting lies and clowning, throwing money from the top of gold buildings. The gold turned out to be fake and so did the money, yet the fat crowd below him kept grunting for more.

There were fake fifties and hundreds stuffed in the man's mouth. Fake twenties were falling from his pockets, but his fatness made it all so confusing. Which bulge was which bulge? Was it fat or was it money?

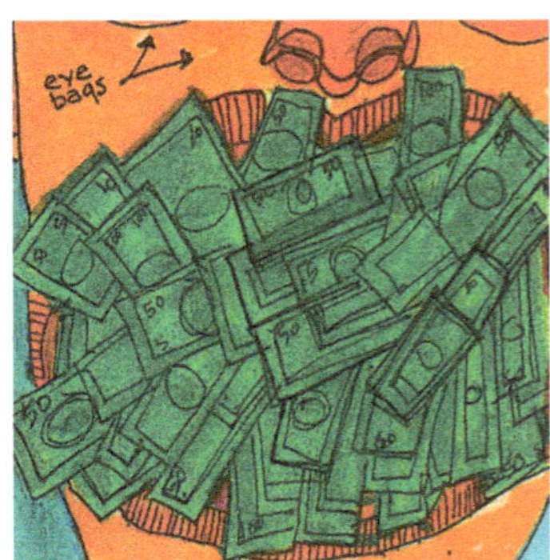

The man's words rubbed together. The friction gave them a shine, like an old suit. But they could look glossy, like marbles, when the sun shone. They caught the eye as if they were worth something. But they weren't worth a damn.

"What if our country falls from the sky and nobody notices but the crows?" I asked my husband, while we were sitting on the couch. "What if the crows come together with their flapping and cawing and cover everything like a thick moss or a fungus? Like now. Is this a warning?"

"What?" he said. Disappointed, I returned to looking for barbarians. I am always looking for barbarians. I don't think there are any on my block. And luckily, my husband's not one.

Bubbles

I heard the bath bubbles' final cries, their tiny pop pop pops. I'm not kidding. I was trying as hard as I could to be mindful. (Defeats the whole purpose, the trying, I know.) For the first time in sixty-nine years, though, I considered the life cycle of the bubble. My husband was downstairs baking bacon, grating cheese. A warm bath, bubbles, eggs, cheese— one of the softest moments of my life.

Acknowledgments

I would like to thank poet Barbara LaMorticella for her expert editorial advice in helping me put together *My Husband's Eyebrows.* I would also like to thank the members of my poetry critique group—Penelope Schott, Suzanne Sigafoos, Tim Barnes and Donna Prinzmetal—for their help in finalizing the writing. And thank you to Sandy Post for that final nudge.

I would also like to thank the following journals for publishing early versions of these poems, sometimes under a different title.

Burningword Literary Journal, Cirque: "My Husband's Eyebrows"

Coal Hill Review: "The Question of Sobbing and Shitting" and "Unbearable Lightness of Marriage"

Your Impossible Voice: "On a Scale of One to Ten," "Compare an Orange," and "Oy"

The Opiate: "Not Invited to the Party"

Florida Review: "Ghost of Our Lust" (as "Ghost of Our Love")

Epoch: "Millionth Crow Poem"

Hole in the Head Review: "Compare an Orange" and "Exactly" (as "But")

great weather for media: "Prequel" (as "Cliché")

Praise for My Husband's Eyebrows

Maintaining that "opposition is the lifeblood," Leanne Grabel takes us on a savvy, sassy, biting history of her thirty-seven-year marriage. She may—as she asserts at one point—always regret each snappish remark, each of her self-described crocodile bites. But we don't. We welcome the rub, the friction, the sparks emanating from this artist's poems and vivid illustrations. What verve! Generously candid and open-hearted, this book gives us its bracing gift: "full spectrum" marital truths that are as irresistible as "the cream in the center of the bon bon."

—Paulann Petersen, Oregon Poet Laureate Emerita

Anyone familiar with Leanne Grabel's writing or her graphic and performing art will recognize the quick and, at times, acid wit, her dance with impulse and anxiety and a demanding sense of independence. What readers of this prose poetical chronicle of her marriage *My Husband's Eyebrows* will find new is how the long trace of time in that marriage imprints a newfound ability to reflect on that past, a broadening sense of trust and even a patience that early in the text she says does not feel capable. Patience, Dante's highest virtue, makes for a beautiful and transformative honesty, a song of acceptance and appreciation: "I thought I'd never see It again/ I mean him in the glint of/ my hunger . . ."

—Charles Seluzicki, author of *Elegiac*

Leanne Grabel bursts out of her box in *My Husband's Eyebrows*, an illustrated chapbook that is a witty, gritty, sometimes hilarious, and always honest examination of her marriage and stages of her life and growth. In language and images that are as exuberant and colorful as fireworks on Independence Day, Leanne shines a new light on her marriage, from the first honeyed sexual encounters to the time, 38 years later, when "My husband and I sit on our brown leather couch like couch pillows. We could probably feed the hungry of a small nation with all the crumbs beneath the cushions."

Leanne opens the book with a Charles Bukowski quote and the lines: "I feel an epiphany coming on." This epiphany is not accompanied by choirs of angels but by the noise of a vacuum as she turns over the couch cushions and cleans out the metaphorical basement: "There are mold spores from the late 19th century down there. They're so old they could be valuable. Or deadly. I'm just happy to see them dying in the new light." In honestly confronting her own anxiety, selfishness, fears, and desires, in probing what in her long marriage is liberating and what is left over from family trauma and from the 19th century, Leanne throws open the marital curtains to let a new light in.

—Barbara LaMorticella, author of *Rain on Waterless Mountain*

If you want to know what life feels like when someone's being honest and funny and insightful and daring—and I mean beyond what you might imagine to be daring and brave and real—here's your book with words and explosively jazzy *a-ha* moment drawings to match. And if you don't want to experience honesty and reality, all the more reason to read the words and dive into the pictures, because this book will open your heart, your mind, and your emotions in ways that you might not expect. Leanne Grabel writes that "candy is absolutely necessary." I would add, this book is absolutely necessary.

—Christopher Beaver, film producer/director

Witty. Fun. Honest. Deeply loving. Unforgivable. Over the top. TMI. Delightful. Did I say loving? Plus, those wild illustrations.

—Penelope Scambly Schott, author of *A is for Anne, Crow Mercies, The Perfect Mother, Sophia & Mister Walter Whitman*, and more

Leanne Grabel's insights, her wry, bright lines and her luscious, hilarious, moody drawings are emotionally resonant, scorchingly honest, and highly entertaining. Grabel pulls back the curtains on marriage—the real and the complex. *My Husband's Eyebrows*, Grabel's illustrated chapbook, should be handed to each and every couple as ink dries on their marriage licenses. After the honeymoon, they can refer to this treatise on marriage as a *long game*, contemplate the gravity of time, and learn about the grit, both coarse and fine, of doubt. Someday, they'll thank her. I thank her, right now, for this illustrated chapbook where text and visuals complement and illuminate each other, like well-seasoned couples.

—Suzanne Sigafoos, author of *This Swarm of Light*

Supposedly there are 36 Questions that when shared between two people seeking intimacy, will lead to love. The 22 poems that comprise *My Husband's Eyebrows* outline what it's like to sustain that love—a love that begins with bathing in warmed honey—golden, thick, and sweet and climbs a rock-hard wall of realization that after 38 years, both of you have become absent listeners whose ears sometimes decide to just get up and go inside.

But, Oh, Sweet Reader, do not despair! No! No! Grabel's tale is a vacation from any familiar version of marital woe. It's a terrifically true story, spoken in words and graphic illustrations over breakfast with white-faced monkeys fanning sugar packets like paper dentures and brimming with observations of electrified eyebrows and thighs, generosity, depression, and shake the rafters loose lust.

Go grab yourself a cocktail, a joint, a warm cup of chai with extra honey, plump up that comfy pillow and start reading. Now.

—Julie Keefe, creative laureate emerita/artist

About the Author / Artist

Leanne Grabel is a writer, illustrator, and performer in love with mixing genres. Her first collaboration was with a bongo player and sax player in the mid-70s and her most recent collaborations were with filmmaker Penny Allen and dancer/choreographer Gregg Bielemeier. She has written & produced numerous multi-media shows, including *The Lighter Side of Chronic Depression* and *Anger: The Musical*. Grabel's graphic novel, *Brontosaurus Illustrated*, recently serialized in *The Opiate*, was published by The Opiate Books in 2022. Grabel is the 2020 recipient of the Bread & Roses Award for contributions to women's literature in the Pacific Northwest. She and her husband started and ran Cafe Lena, a poetry hub and restaurant, throughout the 90s. Grabel is a retired special education teacher, the mother of two daughters and the grandmother of two nubbins, Ophelia and Elliot.

About The Poetry Box®

The Poetry Box, a boutique publishing company in Portland, Oregon, provides a platform for both established and emerging poets to share their words with the world through beautiful printed books and chapbooks.

Feel free to visit the online bookstore (thePoetryBox.com), where you'll find more titles including:

Dear John— by Lauren LeHew

The Catalog of Small Contentments by Carolyn Martin

A Long, Wide Stretch of Calm by Melanie Green

Sophia & Mister Walter Whitman by Penelope Scambly Schott

Of the Forest by Linda Ferguson

Let's Hear It for the Horses by Tricia Knoll

In the Jaguar's House by Debbie Hall

A Nest in the Heart by Vivienne Popperl

Transition Thunderstorms by Beth Bonness

Sitting in Powell's Watching Burnside Dissolve in Rain by Doug Stone

Beneath the Gravel Weight of Stars by Mimi German

Tell Her Yes by Ann Farley

Olympic by John L. Miller

The Weight of Clouds by Cathy Cain

Earthwork by Kristin Berger

Blood Moon by Elaine S. Nussbaum

This Is the Lightness by Rachel Barton

and more . . .